Black. A Coloring |
is dedicated to Black folx all over the world.

Let these pages inspire you to:

Be bold.
Be inspired.
Be unapologetic.
Be intentional.
Be fearless.
Be loud.
Be proud.
Be you.

Make everyone else adjust.

www.blackacoloringbook.com

Every image was AI generated, and inspired by my original, and creative thoughts, with the goal of creating a work that brings joy, deepens imagination, and reminds you of the intricate beauty that is **BLACK**.

I would love to see your masterpieces!

Post pics and reels to your socials and use the following hashtags:

#BlackAColoringBook
#MelanIntentions
#BlackFolxSelfCare

Let's build community!

@melanintentions

Black Artist Spotlight

One thing I will always do is create space for folx who have created space for me!

Scan the QR Code or visit the website to get to know the works of

Takeisha Jefferson.
(Photographer | Artist | Author | Veteran)

www.takeishas.com

My melanin is a gift; it represents strength, resilience, and the legacy of my ancestors. I honor and cherish it every day.

I am black, beautiful, and limitless. My potential reaches as far as my dreams can take me.

The color of my skin is not a barrier but a passport to a legacy of resilience, strength, and excellence.

My melanin enriches me. It fills me with power, strength, and the wisdom of generations.

The richness of my skin color is a testament to my uniqueness, and I honor it by being the best version of myself.

My skin is a tribute to my ancestry, and in its richness, I see hope. It reminds me of my capacity to overcome, to thrive, and to carve out a future as luminous as the stars.

My blackness is not a limitation; it's an expression of beauty and power.

Made in United States
Troutdale, OR
12/05/2023

15375025R00058